CONTENTS

KU-740-155

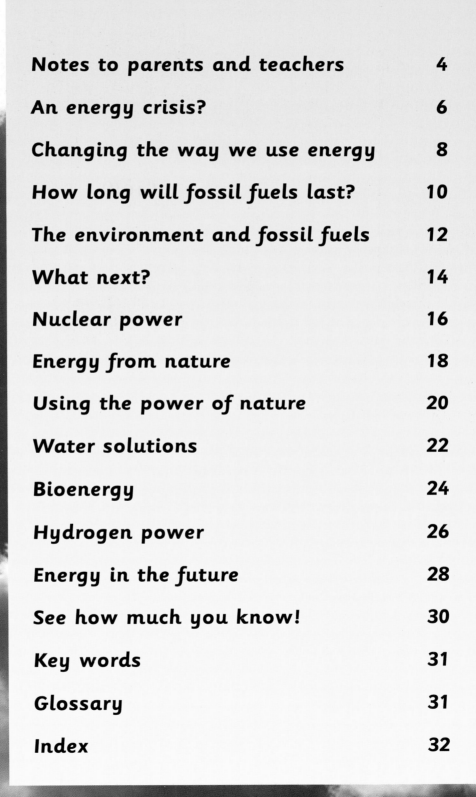

Notes to parents and teachers

This series has been developed for group use in the classroom as well as for children reading on their own. In particular, its differentiated text allows children of mixed abilities to enjoy reading about the same topic. The larger size text (A, below) offers apprentice readers a simplified text. This simplified text is used in the introduction to each chapter and in the picture captions. This font is part of the © Sassoon family of fonts recommended by the National Literacy Early Years Strategy document for maximum legibility. The smaller size text (B, below) offers a more challenging read for older or more able readers.

Bioenergy

All life on Earth depends on the Sun for energy. Much of this energy is stored within plants and animals.

 A

◀ *If plants are replaced then the supply of bioenergy is endless.*

Burning logs to release energy produces gases such as carbon dioxide. However, plants absorb carbon dioxide as they grow.

B

Future Energy

By Rob Bowden

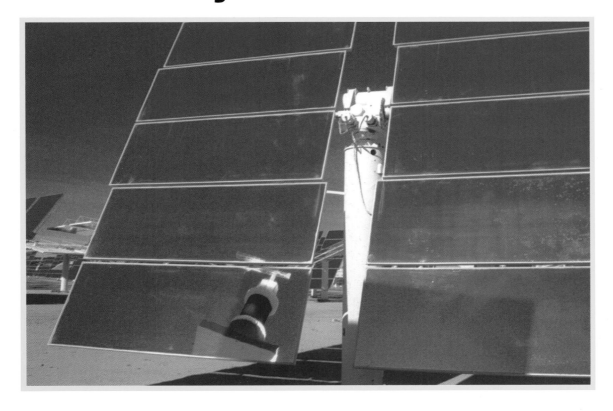

Aladdin/Watts

London • Sydney

PAPERBACK EDITION PRINTED 2008

© Aladdin Books Ltd 2006
Designed and produced by
Aladdin Books Ltd
2/3 Fitzroy Mews
London W1T 6DF

First published in 2006 by
Franklin Watts
338 Euston Road
London NW1 3BH

Franklin Watts Australia
Level 17/207 Kent Street
Sydney NSW 2000

Franklin Watts is a division of
Hachette Children's Books

A catalogue record for this
book is available from the
British Library.

Dewey Classification: 333.79

ISBN 978 0 7496 8154 8

Printed in Malaysia

Editor:
Katie Harker

Design:
Simon Morse
Flick, Book Design and Graphics

Consultant:
Jackie Holderness – former Senior
Lecturer in Primary Education,
Westminster Institute,
Oxford Brookes University

Illustrations:
Simon Morse

Picture researcher:
Alexa Brown

Photocredits:
*l-left, r-right, b-bottom, t-top, c-centre,
m-middle.* Front cover, Back cover, 4t, 6tr,
9tl, 24tl, 31t – Corbis. 1, 15m, 15b, 16bl,
18tr, 20bl, 27tl, 29tl, 30mr – US Department
of Energy. 2-3, 3tl, 3mtl, 3mbl, 6bl, 7bl, 8tl,
9br, 10tr, 10bl, 11tr, 11bl, 12bl, 14tr, 14bl,
15t, 16tr, 17tr, 19tr, 20tl, 21tl, 21br, 22tr,
25tl, 26tl, 26bl, 31b – www.istockphoto.com.
3bl, 28tl, 28bl – NASA. 4b, 13tl, 13br, 24tl,
25br – Photodisc. 7tr – Karen Winton. 8bl –
supplied by the National Insulation
Association. 10br, 30tr – Zach Reinhart. 12tl
– Adam Hart-Davis. 17bl – Select Pictures.
18bl, 30br – John Deere. 19bl – Digital Stock.
22bl – Corel.

Questions, key words and glossary

Each spread ends with a question which parents and teachers can use to discuss and develop further ideas and concepts. Further questions are provided in a quiz on page 30. A reduced version of pages 30 and 31 is shown below. The illustrated 'Key words' section is provided as a revision tool, particularly for apprentice readers, in order to help with spelling, writing and guided reading as part of the literacy hour. The glossary is for more able or older readers. In addition to the glossary's role as a reference aid, it is also designed to reinforce new vocabulary and provide a tool for further discussion and revision. When glossary terms first appear in the text, they are highlighted in bold.

 See how much you know!

Why do we need to stop using fossil fuels?

How long will fossil fuels last if we do nothing to protect them?

What can you do to help save energy?

What are the main energy alternatives to fossil fuels?

Why is nuclear power considered a dangerous technology?

How could water and hydrogen solve all of our energy problems?

How could farmers provide energy?

How could space be used to provide electricity for use on Earth?

Key words

Electricity

Coal

A

Energy   **Heating**

Environment   Oil

Pollution

Glossary

Acid rain – Rain that becomes acidic when it mixes with gases released by burning fossil fuels.

Biogas – A gas that is formed as plants rot. Biogas can be used for energy.

Climate – The normal weather conditions of an area.

Fission – The process of splitting an atom's nucleus into two, to release energy.

Fossil fuels – Fuels that form from the fossilised remains of prehistoric plants and animals. Coal, oil and gas are fossil fuels.

Fusion – The process of joining two atoms' nucleii together, to release energy.

B

Global warming – The warming of the Earth caused by gases in the atmosphere trapping heat from the Sun.

Insulation – A material that helps to keep buildings warm and reduce energy use.

Renewable energy – Sources of energy that can be used again, such as wind, water and solar energy.

An energy crisis?

We live in a world which uses more and more energy. We use energy to light our homes and schools, to keep our homes warm and to drive our cars. We can take this energy for granted, but some energy sources are beginning to run out.

◀ **The world demand for energy is growing even faster than its population.**

Since 1971, the world's population has grown by over 65 per cent. There are now 6.4 billion people and we will add another billion people by 2020! In richer countries, the standard of living has improved for many people. More energy is needed because many people now own cars and use electricity at home.

▶ In developing countries, such as China, the demand for energy is growing very quickly.

A person living in the USA uses about eight times more energy than someone living in China and 15 times more than someone in India. However, in the last 30 years, the energy use of the average person in China has doubled.

Are warnings of a future energy crisis really true?

In recent years, scientists have claimed that our use of energy is damaging the environment. They also warn that energy sources are running out. Is there really a crisis? It will all depend on how we use different forms of energy in the future.

 What could be done to avoid an energy crisis?

Changing the way we use energy

One way to avoid an energy crisis is to think about how we use energy. We waste energy every day at home, at school and in factories. There are things we can do to reduce the energy we use and to protect our energy supplies.

◀ Insulating a roof helps to keep heat in a building.

In a typical home in the western world, people can lose a third of their heating energy through the roof and walls. This energy loss can be greatly reduced by using **insulation** in the attic or between the walls. Fitting double- or even triple-glazed windows is another way to reduce heat loss. Saving energy in this way also reduces the cost of heating bills.

◀ Factories sometimes produce, and then waste, enormous amounts of energy.

Industries use large amounts of energy to make things, but they also waste a lot of energy. Many factories produce waste heat, for example. Scientists are trying to find ways to use this wasted heat energy. In Denmark, the waste energy is used to heat homes.

Wearing a jumper reduces the energy needed to heat a home.

Do you ever leave a light on when you have left a room? Do you leave the television on standby when you are not watching it? All of these things waste energy. Think how much energy could be saved if we all changed the way we use energy just a little.

 How could your family reduce the energy they use?

How long will fossil fuels last?

Most of the world's energy comes from fossil fuels such as oil, coal and gas. These fuels are millions of years old and we cannot replace them once we have used them. They are known as non-renewable fuels.

◀ The energy released by burning fossil fuels allows this plane to fly.

Fossil fuels are the remains of ancient plants and animals found underground Over millions of years, heat and pressure changed the rotting remains into coal, oil and gas. When fossil fuels are burned they release heat energy. This can be used to make electricity and to power cars and planes.

▶ Gas provides energy to cook this food, but for how much longer?

Once fossil fuels have been used, they cannot be replaced. Some experts believe the world will run out of oil in around 2045 and that gas supplies will be finished by 2071.

As fossil fuels begin to run out, the price of fuel is expected to rise.

The price of fossil fuels is related to their supply. If supplies are good, the price is low. But as supplies run short, prices begin to rise. Events, such as wars and natural disasters, can also affect the price of oil by disrupting supplies.

 Why can't fossil fuels be replaced easily?

The environment and fossil fuels

Burning fossil fuels releases gases that pollute the air around us. The gases can be harmful to nature. They can also combine with water in the air to form acid rain. This causes stone buildings and statues to crumble.

◀ Factories that burn fossil fuels release polluting gases into the air.

Carbon dioxide is one of these gases. It traps energy from the Sun. This is making the Earth warmer and causing our **climate** to change. Many people call this change **global warming**. Sulphur dioxide is another polluting gas. It mixes with water in the clouds and falls as **acid rain** that damages nature and buildings.

◀ **Environments can be badly damaged by pipelines carrying fossil fuels.**

Some fossil fuels are in remote and delicate environments. Building pipelines for the fuels can be very destructive. In Cameroon, in Africa, large areas of rainforest have been destroyed to build an oil pipeline across the country.

Are the effects of this hurricane a warning from nature?

Many parts of the world have been damaged by our use of energy. In northern Europe, for example, acid rain has destroyed forests. Very severe storms have also caused damage around the world. Many scientists think that these storms are a result of global warming.

 Can you think of any examples of our climate changing?

What next?

Solving the world's energy problems is very difficult. We need to protect the environment by reducing our use of fossil fuels. This means making changes to the way energy is used. Businesses may also have to change, affecting the jobs that people do.

◀ There is energy all around us that we could use.

The Sun, the wind and the oceans can all make cleaner energy that we can use. We can also use plants to make energy. These natural resources offer endless supplies of alternative energy. We need to find a way to capture this energy so that it is cheap and easy to use.

There are three main alternatives to fossil fuels.

Nuclear power

Scientists are looking for cheap sources of energy that do not cause pollution. Nuclear power (see page 16) is likely to become a very important source of energy in the coming years. Natural energy sources, such as wind, tidal and solar power (see pages 18-25), are also being developed. If enough energy can be captured from these sources, they will be a useful supply of **renewable energy**. Hydrogen gas (see page 26) is also thought to become a clean source of fuel for the future. But in the meantime, we need to reduce the amount of energy that we use. We will still need to use fossil fuels for some years, so we need to reduce the impact that burning them has on the environment.

Energy from nature

Hydrogen gas

 What should be the energy priorities for the future?

Nuclear power

Nuclear power produces large amounts of energy, but nuclear fuels are harmful to people and wildlife. Nuclear experts say that modern power stations are safe, but many people believe the risk of an accident is too great.

◀ **Nuclear fuel releases enormous amounts of energy.**

Nuclear power is generated by forcing atoms of uranium or plutonium to split apart. This is known as nuclear **fission**. The process is carefully controlled in special cooling tanks. The energy released is then used to heat steam for generating electricity.

▶ Nuclear power stations generate about 17 per cent of the world's electricity.

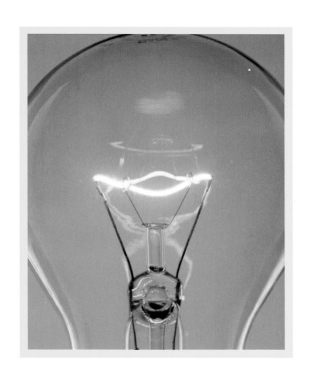

Nuclear power produces a lot of energy without releasing polluting gases. Some countries, such as France, use a lot of nuclear energy. Other countries are looking at using nuclear power for a cleaner energy future.

Nuclear accidents are rare, but very damaging.

Nuclear fuels give off radiation that can make people or wildlife very ill. Nuclear waste remains radioactive for thousands of years. It is difficult to know how to safely store this waste. This concrete structure was built to cover nuclear waste caused by an accident at Chernobyl, Ukraine.

 Why are houses near to a nuclear power station unpopular?

Energy from nature

Scientists have found some solutions for cleaner energy. These alternatives are less damaging to the environment. The challenge now is how to persuade governments to consider using these new forms of energy.

◄ **Farmers could soon be harvesting energy as well as food.**

In the future, we must work with nature instead of against it. Growing crops to make biofuels (see page 24) is a good example. Although these fuels still release carbon dioxide when they are burnt, they absorb carbon dioxide as they grow. This balances the amount of carbon dioxide in the atmosphere.

▶ Future gas supplies could come from seaweed.

Nature often provides scientists with surprising energy solutions. Sea kelp is a type of seaweed that grows up to 60 centimetres a day. Sea kelp could be farmed and converted into **biogas** as a renewable source of energy.

Governments have agreed to reduce pollution from fossil fuels.

Government support is needed to encourage renewable energy sources. The UK government, for example, has reduced taxes for clean energy users. More money is also needed to research cleaner sources of energy.

 Which alternative energy do you think we should research?

Using the power of nature

Almost all our energy comes from nature. Even fossil fuels come from the remains of ancient plants and animals. However, there is much more that could be done to use renewable energy sources, such as the power of the Sun and the wind.

◀ **These panels capture the energy of the Sun.**

When you feel the heat of the Sun on your skin you are experiencing solar energy. Special panels can capture this energy and use it to provide heat or to generate electricity. Solar energy works best in sunny countries, such as Spain or Australia, but can be used almost anywhere. The newest solar panels can even be made into roof tiles.

◀ Wind energy is cheap and easy to use.

Sail boats and windmills have used the energy of the wind for hundreds of years. Modern wind turbines catch the wind's energy and turn it into electricity. Wind turbines are often placed together in wind farms, but some people think they spoil the landscape.

Heat in the centre of the Earth can give us energy.

Deep underground there is a massive store of heat energy. In some places this energy is found close to the Earth's surface and can be used. In Iceland, water pipes pass through hot rocks to provide homes with hot water.

 In what ways do you use the energy of the Sun or the wind?

Water solutions

Most of the Earth's surface is covered in water. This water contains enormous amounts of energy from crashing waves and thundering waterfalls. Less than one per cent of the energy in the world's oceans could provide four times more energy than we currently use.

◄ **Large dams store water to generate electricity.**

Many of the world's rivers have dams built across them to store water for generating electricity. The water is sent through turbines that spin as the water passes, to generate electricity. This electricity is called hydro-electric power.

Tides contain enormous amounts of energy.

Special turbines, a bit like underwater wind farms, can be used to capture tidal energy. Alternatively, a barrier can be placed across a bay or a river. The water passes through gates in the barrier. This contains turbines linked to generators that make electricity.

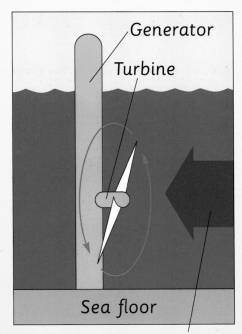

Generator
Turbine
Sea floor
Tide coming in

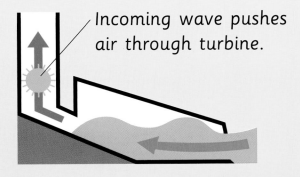

Incoming wave pushes air through turbine.

New technology allows us to use wave energy to make electricity.

Wave energy is often destructive so using it can be difficult. An oscillating water column (OWC) uses the energy of waves to force air in and out of a column. As the air moves, it spins a turbine to generate electricity.

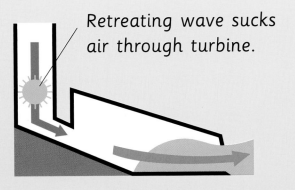

Retreating wave sucks air through turbine.

Why might water be a good source of future energy?

Bioenergy

All life on Earth depends on the Sun for energy. Much of this energy is stored within plants and animals and can be used. Burning a log, for example, is simply releasing energy stored by the tree when it was growing. We call this bioenergy.

◀ If plants are replaced then the supply of bioenergy is endless.

Burning logs to release energy produces gases such as carbon dioxide. However, plants absorb carbon dioxide as they grow. This means that if we plant trees at the same rate as we cut them for fuel, the environment will not suffer. Other plant-based fuels also provide a renewable energy source in this way.

◀ Sugar cane is high in energy.

In Brazil, a fuel called ethanol is made from sugar cane and used instead of petrol to fuel cars. Biodiesel is another fuel made from crops such as corn, sunflowers or soybeans. Biodiesel and ethanol are much cleaner than oil-based fuels and are also renewable.

Waste material releases gases that can be used for energy.

When plants or animals decompose they release gases. This biogas can be collected to use as an energy source. In Stockholm in Sweden, rubbish is used to produce biogas for cooking and heating. Biogas can also be collected from landfill sites.

 Why is bioenergy a renewable source of energy?

Hydrogen power

Scientists think that hydrogen gas could provide us with an endless and clean supply of energy to meet all our future energy needs. The problem is that hydrogen has to be made first. This uses a lot of energy.

◀ **Water contains hydrogen that could be the fuel of the future.**

Many things contain hydrogen, including fossil fuels, but the most exciting source of hydrogen is water. Water is made of hydrogen and oxygen. Hydrogen can be separated from water using a process called electrolysis, with oxygen as the only waste gas. Electrolysis needs a lot of energy, however, so it is expensive to use.

◀ **Hydrogen fuel cells are used to power this car.**

When hydrogen is used in a fuel cell the opposite of electrolysis occurs. The hydrogen mixes with oxygen and produces energy (with water as a waste product). Fuel cells could be used for domestic and industrial purposes, but so far their main use has been in transport.

Energy can also be made by combining atoms.

Nuclear fission (see page 16) makes energy by splitting atoms. Nuclear **fusion** joins atoms together. This technology could be a cheaper source of energy to power the electrolysis needed to extract hydrogen from water.

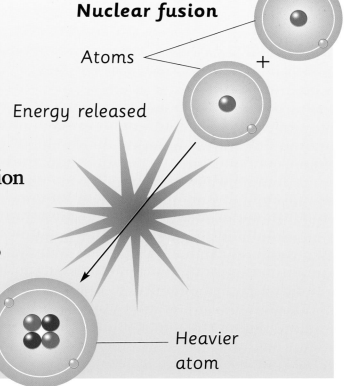

Nuclear fusion

Atoms

+

Energy released

Heavier atom

 Why is hydrogen a good source of renewable energy?

Energy in the future

Fifty years ago the thought of driving a car on hydrogen fuel made from water was just a dream. Today it can be done. In another fifty years, perhaps we'll use the Sun to power our cars and we'll capture most of our energy from space?

◀ **Space could be the ultimate energy source for Earth.**

Solar power is already used in space to power spacecraft and satellites. Soon however, solar satellites could gather solar energy and use microwave beams to send it back to Earth. The beam could then be converted into electricity to supply endless clean energy.

◀ Solar power has great potential for the future.

The amount of energy reaching the Earth from the Sun is around 10,000 times the world's current demand. In South Africa and the USA, scientists are developing solar panels that can be printed onto paper. Cars and buildings could also use solar power.

Energy from the oceans can make electricity.

The world's oceans absorb energy from the Sun. This makes surface waters much warmer than deep waters. Ocean Thermal Energy Conversion (OTEC) uses the difference in temperatures to generate electricity.

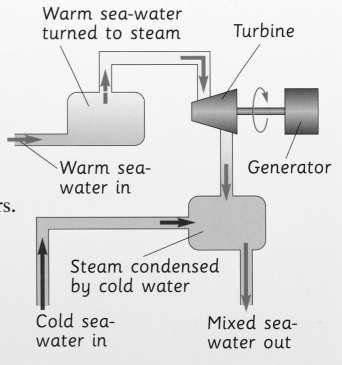

Warm sea-water turned to steam

Turbine

Warm sea-water in

Generator

Steam condensed by cold water

Cold sea-water in

Mixed sea-water out

 What would life be like without new sources of energy?

Why do we need to stop using fossil fuels?

How long will fossil fuels last if we do nothing to protect them?

What can you do to help save energy?

What are the main energy alternatives to fossil fuels?

Why is nuclear power considered a dangerous technology?

How could water and hydrogen solve all of our energy problems?

How could farmers provide energy?

How could space be used to provide electricity for use on Earth?

Key words

Electricity

Coal   Gas
Energy   Heating
Environment   Oil
Fuel   Population

Pollution

Glossary

Acid rain – Rain that becomes acidic when it mixes with gases released by burning fossil fuels.

Biogas – A gas that is formed as plants rot. Biogas can be used for energy.

Climate – The normal weather conditions of an area.

Fission – The process of splitting an atom's nucleus into two, to release energy.

Fossil fuels – Fuels that form from the fossilised remains of prehistoric plants and animals. Coal, oil and gas are fossil fuels.

Fusion – The process of joining two atoms' nucleii together, to release energy.

Global warming – The warming of the Earth caused by gases in the atmosphere trapping heat from the Sun.

Insulation – A material that helps to keep buildings warm and reduce energy use.

Renewable energy – Sources of energy that can be used again, such as wind, water and solar energy.

Index